HOW TO CHANGE
YOUR AMAZON
PASSWORD ON
YOUR KINDLE

An Easy & Trusted Approach to Changing Your Amazon Password on Your Kindle and Other Devices, Including Clearer Pictures + Easy Password Cracking; *(You Must Not Be a Professional)*

By

ENGR.WILEY LOUIS

TABLE OF CONTENTS

CHAPTER ONE

How to change password on your Amazon account

CHAPTER TWO

How to crack password of an account

PROCEDURES

- Applying guessing approach
- Try and access the password manager
- Apply the password reset links

CHAPTER ONE

HOW TO CHANGE PASSWORD ON YOUR AMAZON ACCOUNT

Password is refer to a string of character that is use to verify if the user a computer / system is the authenticated person .it is also a security code which can either be in numeric, alphabetic and alphanumeric

Change of password arises as a result of security treat to your Amazon account.

Here is a simplify steps on how to create a new password on your Amazon account with the use of android device.

PROCEDURES

1. You are to open the Amazon shopping application through

your android: looking at your application menu, you we see a white square icon which looks like a shopping cart.

✓ In case your Amazon is not automatically logged, click on the orange button thereby signing in with your recognized email and password.

2. You will now tap the icon on your screen displaying three horizontal lines.

✓ This icon is displayed at the upper corner of your android.

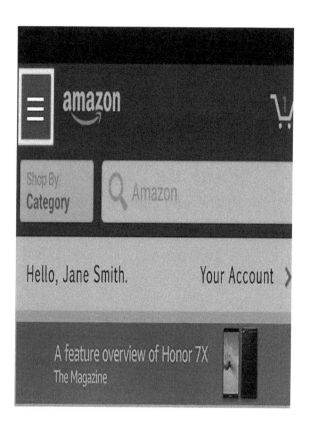

Immediately, your navigation panel will open on the left hand side of your device.

Your Orders

Your Wish List

Your Account

Amazon Pay

Try Prime

3. On your navigation panel, click on "YOUR ACCOUNT". Once this is done, a new page will display showing account settings as seen below.

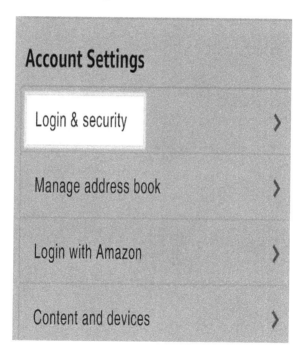

4. Below the account settings is an icon showing "LOGIN & SECURITY", click on it.

Once this is done, a new page will be seen having your name, phone, email and password settings.

5. Click on the "EDIT BUTTON" which is close to your password box. This option is located at the lower part of your login & security menu. This area is where access to creating a new password is achieved.

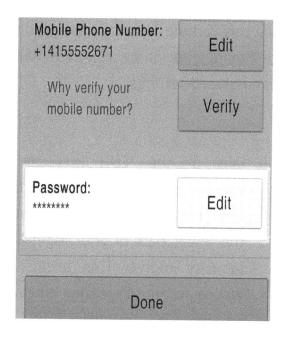

6. PASSWORD FIELD WILL BE
   DISPLAYED. You are expected
   to enter correctly your current
   password.

   ✓ On this field, Tap the
     change password page and
     enter correctly the

password you are using
before.

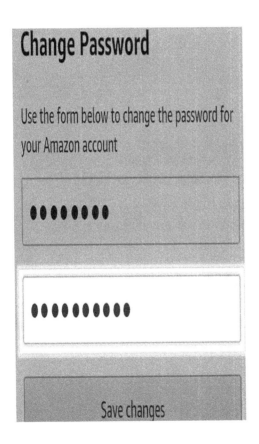

Change Password

Use the form below to change the password for
your Amazon account

●●●●●●●●

●●●●●●●●●●

Save changes

7. NEW PASSWORD FIELD WILL
   BE DISPLAYED. CLICK ON THIS
   FIELD AND ENTER A NEW
   PASSWORD FOR YOUR
   ACCOUNT

8. Click on the orange color
   display, displaying "save

change''. Once this is done, your new password is save thereby overriding the other password. Sign in will now be possible using your new password.

CHAPTER TWO

HOW TO CRACK PASSWORD OF AN ACCOUNT

PROCEDURES ONE

APPLYING GUESSING APPROACH

STEPS:

A. USING THE ACCOUNT HOLDER COMPUTER: getting the password will be easier if you have free access to the account holder computer because he/she might store its commonly used password somewhere in the system.

- ✓ Go to the search bar using your cursor to search documents within your personal computer. Macs systems uses Finder app. The keys words you will search for are "account" and "user name" or "user name", and password".

- ✓ Make sure you take some time to search for any hidden files.

B. PUT DOWN VITAL INFORMATION OF THE ACCOUNT CREATOR: this vital information can be date of birth, pets name, spouse name and others which will aid us in answering any security question that will arise during the password search.

- ✓ Their spouse name plus their phone number can be their used password.

C. YOU ARE TO USE ANY VITAL INFORMATION YOU KNOW ABOUT THE PASSWORD CREATOR

Try to use anything you know about the password creator to guess the likely password. Here are some helpful guides to getting vital information about the password creator:

- PASSWORD CREATOR PERSONAL INFORMATION: example is their pet name. if the security questions are gotten and enter correctly, it will help in bypassing the password.

- DETAILS FROM SOCIAL MEDIA: if you are a close friend to the person on social media or you know his likes and interest, this might reflects answers to his security question.

John Smith like this.

D. ASK ANYBODY CLOSER TO THE PASSWORD CREATOR THAT KNOWS THE PASSWORD: this might be possible especially when you are the boss or parent to the person having the account. Such password can be release to you when you what to know all that is happening around such persons account so as to be able to get better facts.

PROCEDURE TWO

TRY AND ACCESS THE PASSWORD MANAGER

STEPS

A. CHECK TO CONFIRM IF A PASSWORD MANAGER WAS USED BY THE PASSWORD CREATOR

This can be accessed by typing "password manager" in the search bar of your personal computer (finder app for Macs). For this services, ("Google and face book") password manager normally store password that are commonly used

Below is the list of common password managers:

- ✓ Store Browser Information

- ✓ Keychain
- ✓ Google Smart Lock

B. YOU WILL NOW OPEN THE PASSWORD MANAGER

It is notice that the password manager is password protected in several cases. In case you know the password, other saved password can then be viewed and applied to the respective services.

- Auto fill data is what you will depend on in the case when you don't have access to the password in viewing the website/program you need.

C. ENTER AN ACCOUNT USER NAME.

From your selected browser, a password may automatically be generated for you if the account you are about to login has a saved password on the browser. This automatic password generation will only be possible when you enter the username correctly.

- When the autofill and cookies are enabled, Mozilla Firefox and Google chrome will generate the password for you.
- For account holder using Macs computer having the keychain password will assist you in getting the stored password. In the utilities folder,
  - ➢ click on Keychain Access
  - ➢ click to open the password tab located at the left side of your screen
  - ➢ select the desire password you want

You might desire to display the password in a plain text style.

PROCEDURE THREE

APPLY THE PASSWORD RESET LINKS

A. TAKE YOUR CURSOR AND CLICK FORGOT PASSWORD

This action is located below the password field.

B. **AT THIS TIME, YOUR PASSWORD RECOVERY OPTION SHOULD BE REVIEWED.** Below are the several ways by which your password could be reset:

- By receiving SMS alert of your password link on your phone
- By receiving email messages of your password link
- By answering all the security question

C. MAKE SURE ALL THE NECESSARY INFORMATION NEEDED TO RESET THE PASSWORD IS WITH YOU

It is expected that vital information about the password creator already resides in you. Failure that his vital information means you will try and get a physical contact with his phone or email address.

- If the password creator uses an IOS device that is synchronized to the computer you are currently using, it will enable you to see the password reset link from Macs messages. Immediate you alter the password of the creator, it automatically alert him/her that something fraudulent is happening to his password. This procedure is risky

C. ALL ON-SCREEN INSTRUCTION SHOULD BE FOLLOWED CORRECTLY.

If you know that you have all it takes to receive the reset link after answering all the security questions, it indicates that resetting the password and gaining access into the account becomes easier.

THE END